Will anything happen if I pray?

GW00724626

PETER GRAYSTONE

The Lord is near to
all who call on him;
to all who call on him
in truth.

From the Bible: Psalm 145 verse 18

Contents

Everybody asks...

Prayer is easy. So easy. You just talk to God, and God listens. Always!

Surely everybody in the world has prayed at some point in their lives. People find that they can't help themselves.

It might happen in an emergency when you feel you need all the help you can get, even though you don't think about God very often in other circumstances.

It might happen at a moment of great joy and excitement like the birth of a baby. You find yourself thanking everybody on earth, but you are still so thrilled that you start thanking everybody in heaven as well.

A cathedral or a beautiful church is also a place where people have an urge to pray. Something about the beauty and the stillness reminds you that Christians have prayed to God in that place for centuries. The richness of all that faith curls around in the peaceful air. Your mind drifts beyond the walls to think about the source of love and wonder and life itself. That's a prayer too!

Prayer feels good. It seems the natural thing to do in those circumstances. But the question is: Will anything happen if I pray?

When I stopped praying, coincidences stopped happening.

William Temple, Archbishop of Canterbury, 1881-1944

Christians believe...

Christians follow the way of Jesus, who lived about 2,000 years ago in the lands now shared by Israel and Palestine. His message was that God wants to lead men and women from despair to hope, from darkness to light. He told people of the great love God has for them. Broken people found hope. Suffering people experienced healing. Brutalised people glimpsed justice.

Jesus taught his followers to talk to God in the same way that he did – like a child speaks to an adoring father. Simple! But also awesome, because when you pray you are in the presence of the God who is almighty, the creator of everything that has ever existed.

So when you pray you are putting yourself in touch with the maker and shaper of the world's destiny. You can lay before God your deepest hope, your greatest happiness, and all your anxieties. And you can open yourself to God directing and changing you.

But God's love for the world is so great that he is not only interested in grand ideas. He registers and responds to all kinds of prayers. That includes a desperate cry in a crisis, rage following a tragedy, or a vague grunt by someone who has barely even thought about whether he exists.

So what is a prayer? Is it a request that God will change the world in the way you personally want him to?

Well... not really.

A better way of looking at it is as an active way of participating in the way God works out his plan for the world. Very often God's answer to a prayer is a change in your own attitudes or actions.

But having said that, there are occasions when the result of a prayer is that something happens, which seems to show that God has intervened miraculously. And then there is every reason to be thrilled.

So if your friend has got an interview tomorrow for a job that she really needs, go ahead and pray about it. Be honest about what you hope for. God will be overjoyed to hear from you. That is his nature.

Pray, and let God do the worrying.

Martin Luther, a German priest whose actions had a world-changing impact on the Christian church, 1483-1546

Prayer can involve words or silence.

You can say prayers aloud or think them in your head.

You can pray as an individual or in a group - for instance together in a church.

You can read prayers that someone else has written. There are many books containing beautiful words that Christians (and before them Jews, who pray to the same God) have written over the course of hundreds of years.

However, you can also use your own words, which are extremely meaningful even if they don't feel very poetic.

And there are scores of creative ways you can pray - through art, through music, or by lighting a candle. There really are no rules. Some people find it helpful to focus by making use of a string of beads (a rosary) which they feed through their fingers as they pray.

In many ways, praying is as straightforward as having a conversation. And just like conversations, some people take to it naturally and some people wonder what on earth to say.

The next few pages are about things that Christians feel they want to say to God. Usually it is a pleasure for them to do so. A serious pleasure, but a pleasure nevertheless.

Praising

This involves putting into words (or even into song) how great you think God is.

You can focus on the wonder of all he has created, or the immensity of his power, or the intricacy of his care for every detail of each living thing. God is utterly holy, loving and just. He is awesome and yet endlessly compassionate.

Praise acknowledges that and takes joy in it. It means taking an appropriate position of humility in front of God and then being thrilled that such a vast and eternal being knows you by name.

It is equally fulfilling to turn your thoughts about the greatness of God into an absence of words. Simply to gaze on something beautiful, either in a natural landscape or in a piece of art, and to let your mind fill with notions and emotions about the creator of all things is a meaningful act of praise.

Your mind boggles at the thought of God who is ancient before all time, vast beyond all existence and mysterious beyond all knowledge. But surprisingly, this doesn't make you feel feeble. Instead it fills you with a sense of the dignity of being a human, for the God you are praising knows you by name.

Of course, when you praise God you shouldn't feel limited to using the word 'he'. Because God is infinite, gender is meaningless and human languages will never be sufficient.

Thanking

This is a way of recognising that everything which gives value or joy to life is the gift of a Creator, not just good fortune. Christians don't get into the habit of thanking God because they become religious; they do it because they become grateful. When that happens, it becomes instinctive.

It's usual for Christians to thank God for things which bring a sense of enjoyment to life, such as music, beauty, sex and possessions. And very often prayers of thanks take in spiritual blessings, such as having peace or knowing that you are loved by God.

The end of a day is a point at which looking back with thankfulness seems natural. God doesn't have a crotchety character which is ill-humoured if he is not thanked. Rather, those who consistently thank God develop a sense of satisfaction with life because they are increasingly aware of the good things which enrich it.

Another point at which Christians frequently thank God is immediately before a meal. It is usually done while the food is in front of them, with its enticing smells and colours. This is called 'saying grace'. Its origins are older than Christianity and Jesus, like other Jews, is recorded as giving thanks to God before meals.

Asking

Prayers of this kind can be personal (such as begging for healing for a sick relative) or immense in scale (such as longing for the end of a war). They can be individual or shared, spontaneous or planned. Very often they are silent prayers which a person thinks about or puts into words in the privacy of their room.

Saying a prayer is not the same as making a wish. Making a wish puts you at the mercy of a tumultuous universe. Praying is a focussed way of seeking the help of a gracious God.

When prayers such as these take place while a group is gathered together, they are sometimes called 'intercessions'. In these circumstances one person generally says a prayer aloud, or reads it, and at its close the rest of the group responds with the Latin word 'Amen', which means 'Yes indeed!'

A search for guidance and help very often features in prayers of this kind. It's very common to ask God for direction, or to seek understanding in the face of the mysteries involved in being alive.

There appears to be no limit to what it is acceptable to ask God to do, and Jesus encouraged his followers to believe that God would answer. He taught that God would always respond to prayer in the way which best works out his purposes for the entire world.

Every Christian is aware, however, that the result of a prayer is not always the outcome they hoped for. Miracles have been known, but great disappointments have been known as well. Attempting to twist God's arm to achieve your desired result seems to be neither possible nor desirable.

Asking for forgiveness

One of the elements of the Christian faith that believers find most precious is that God is endlessly willing to forgive.

We are aware of our personal failings, which can be trivial or serious. We are also aware of worldwide injustice and wickedness, such as racism or the damage humans are doing to the environment. The writers of the Bible call any failure to follow God's way 'sin.'

Asking for forgiveness begins by recognising that we have done wrong, either because what we have done has hurt someone or because it has contributed in some way to global wrongdoing. But it also involves a genuine willingness to change your ways as evidence that you are sorry. That desire to turn around is called 'repentance'.

It releases God's mercy instantly, unstintingly and with no exceptions. For some people this brings a sense of relief and joy. For others there is just a quiet knowledge that they have done the right thing. In some circumstances, that opportunity for a new start can be life-changing.

Admitting your wrongdoing and receiving God's forgiveness is a very sensitive thing and for some it is best done alone and in private. Others find themselves helped by making a confidential confession to a priest, usually in a church building, where they can hear a whispered assurance that God forgives them.

Worshipping in a church

Christians make a habit of gathering together to pray to God. Very often this is on a Sunday, because that was the day when Jesus rose from the dead. It's called 'worship', which comes from an Old English word that means telling someone how much they are worth to you.

A service in a church building usually features all the kinds of prayer that have been listed so far. Much of it is set to music, especially the praise. Saying sorry to God, and asking for his help, can seem more intense when you have the encouragement of others around you sharing the experience.

Another feature of public worship is saying aloud together the things that Christians believe, especially about Jesus. There are several short statements of belief in the Bible, which are sometimes used. But it is more common to say 'creeds' which come from the centuries immediately after Jesus lived. A creed is a kind of a prayer because worshippers are speaking to God, but they are also declaring to each other that this faith shapes their lives.

Frequently worship comes to a climax with everyone eating bread and drinking wine. This practice follows an unbroken tradition back through the centuries to the night before Jesus died. He asked his followers to do this in order to remember him. It recognises that Jesus's death and resurrection are central to a Christian's relationship with God. The bread is a symbol of Jesus's body broken when he was crucified; the wine represents the blood shed as he died. Whether it's known as Communion, Eucharist or Mass, this too is an offering of prayer.

Church services can be quiet or noisy, or have elements of both. A feature of some churches, but not all, is ecstatic prayer in which an individual or an entire congregation speaks in a language that is not recognisable to them. The Spirit of God enables them to praise him in ways that bypass human language. It is sometimes followed by an interpretation into the local language. This is known as 'speaking in tongues' or 'praying in the Spirit'.

Contemplating God

Many Christians also find deep value in setting aside time to be still and to become attentive to God's presence. Meditating in this way, they become increasingly aware of the meaning of their place on earth. They sense a shape for their lives in which they and God are in partnership, and they become alert to the divine love which gives worth to existence.

Silence helps people find a comfortable stillness when they pray in this way. It can be done either individually or together as a group. Often people turn a word or phrase over and over in their mind, not so much to analyse its meaning as to allow it to work on their imagination. It could be a phrase from the Bible such as 'God is love' or even a single word such as 'Jesus'.

Praying in a crisis

If you haven't got time to think about what kind of prayer is appropriate, just tell God how it is. Right there; right then! You will be heard.

'I know the plans I have for you,' declares the Lord, 'plans to prosper you and not to harm you, plans to give you hope and a future. Then you will call on me and come and pray to me, and I will listen to you.'

From the Bible: Jeremiah chapter 29 verses 11 & 12

When Jesus's followers asked him how they should pray, he taught them words which have proved so helpful to Christians, that in every century and every corner of the world they have been repeated. It is called 'The Lord's Prayer'. Most of it comes from the Bible. The ending comes from a book called The Didache, compiled about 70 years after Jesus's resurrection. It reveals a lot about how Christians prayed nearly 2,000 years ago. They said this prayer three times every day. The themes in the prayer are often used as a pattern for other prayers:

Our Father in heaven,
hallowed be your name,

your kingdom come,
your will be done,
on earth as in heaven.

Give us today our daily bread.

Forgive us our sins
as we forgive those
who sin against us.

Lead us not into temptation,
but deliver us from evil.

For the kingdom, the power,
and the glory are yours
now and for ever.

Amen.

[God] does not ask much of us, merely a thought of him from time to time – a little act of adoration, sometimes to ask for his grace, sometimes to offer him your sufferings, at other times to thank him for the blessings, past and present, he has given you. In the midst of your troubles take comfort in him as often as you can.

Lift up your heart to him during your meals and in company. The least little remembrance will always be the most pleasing to him. One need not cry out very loudly; he is nearer to us than we think.

Brother Lawrence, a French monk whose book 'The Practice of the Presence of God' has never been out of print, 1614-1691

Everything we know about God suggests that he is willing to answer our prayers. But it's obvious that some prayers are answered, and some are not. Why?

Over the years Christians have tried to make sense of the joy, confusion, dismay or relief that they feel when particular things happen after they have prayed for something.

Might it be wrong to assume that 'yes' is the only acceptable answer to a prayer? God may, for reasons that aren't clear from a human perspective, answer 'no' or 'not yet'. Jesus compared God to a wise father who will not give his children things that aren't good for them.

Of course, when terrible pain continues, despite fervent prayers, it's natural to wonder how God can possibly bring anything positive out of such a bad situation. Christian faith has always involved trust that, even when there are disappointments and setbacks, God's plans are ultimately good. But it is quite acceptable to shout out in anger to God when you feel let down - that too is a prayer.

Alternatively, could it be that we are confused by God's response to prayer because he is working on a different timescale? Although it seems from a human perspective that prayer has made no difference, the answer might be experienced some time later.

Sometimes the first time a person prays is in a desperate situation. Many who call out to God receive help in those circumstances. But longing for a particular outcome can sometimes make prayer more like a demand than a request. It can't be right to treat God as if it's a human right to have him carry out our instructions.

Answers to prayer come when we are asking for things that are part of God's agenda, not ours. The more we come to know and love Jesus, the more our thinking lines up with his. Our ways become his ways and our desires his desires.

We have an invitation to step into Jesus's world and stay close to him. The result of that is to see things as he sees them, to want the things that he wants, and to pray for things that God wants to do.

The Lord is near.
Do not be anxious
about anything,
but in every situation,
by prayer and petition,
with thanksgiving, present
your requests to God.
And the peace of God,
which transcends all
understanding, will guard
your hearts and your minds
in Christ Jesus.

From the Bible: Philippians chapter 4 verses 5-7

You could...

How can you go about investigating whether anything happens if you pray? Try one or try them all.

Seek out a quiet place

Tell God your name. Talk about things that are on your mind. Tell him about your life, your hopes, and the people you care for most. Then say 'Amen' like Christians have for centuries, meaning 'Yes indeed!'.

Light a candle and watch the flame flicker

Bring to mind some of the things you have been thinking about God. Include the questions and doubts you have, as well as the thanks and the longings. As you become aware of the heat rising, also be aware that your thoughts are rising to the God who always hears.

Try out a church service

Have a look at their website first and find out whether it's one of the lively ones or one of the quiet ones – choose which you prefer. Sit at the back and copy everyone else. When it comes to the prayers, listen attentively and consider whether they are words you want to echo. See what you make of it.

Read a Psalm

In the Bible there is a collection of prayers called the Psalms. They are Jewish prayers about 3,000 years old, and Jesus knew them well. Read a few and discover whether they include things you want to say to God. You might be surprised to find that there is pain and rage in them, as well as praise and love.

At the end of a day, sit on your bed and think back on what has happened since you woke

Go through the day hour by hour. Has God popped into your mind at any point, or has anything happened which you now think might have had a hint of God in it? Pick out something you are thankful for, something you regret, and something that the world needs (or that you need). Tell God you hope he is listening.

Google 'famous prayers' or borrow a book of Christian prayers from a library.

Take time to go through them, working out whether these time-honoured words chime with what you would like to say to God. If one of them strikes you as particularly beautiful or helpful, copy it out and keep returning to it.

Have a go at praying without any words.

Go outside under a blue sky or a starry night. Look up, and wander about a bit doing nothing in particular. Simply look and think about what the implications would be for your life if God has made it all. See whether any thoughts come to you, which might be interpreted as God communicating with you. Open yourself up to the possibility of God having a bigger part in your life than he has so far. Take a deep breath and tell him you will give faith a go!

Explore more...

The website explorechristianity.info is a portal that can lead you to much more information. It will help you find answers from a Christian point of view to life's biggest questions.

You will find:

- Information about the Christian faith and its founder Jesus Christ

- Suggestions on how to begin living as a Christian

- Ideas to help faith grow

- Advice about meeting other Christians in churches and cathedrals

- Links to reliable websites where you can discover more.

explorechristianity.info

Notes

[Jesus said:] When you pray, go into your room, close the door and pray to your Father, who is unseen.

Then your Father, who sees what is done in secret, will reward you...

Your Father knows what you need before you ask him.

From the Bible: Matthew chapter 6 verses 6-8